Into the Deep

Calling all aliens!

Are you planning a holiday to planet Earth?

Finn and Zeek are here to help.

'Into the Deep'
Published by MAVERICK ARTS PUBLISHING LTD

Suite 1, Hillreed House, 54 Queen Street,
Horsham, RH13 5AD, +44 (0)1403 256941
© Maverick Arts Publishing Limited August 2024

A CIP catalogue record for this book is available at the British Library.

ISBN 978-1-83511-012-6

Printed in India

www.maverickbooks.co.uk

Credits:

Finn & Zeek illustrations by Jake McDonald, Bright Illustration Agency
Cover: Jake McDonald / Bright, © David Shale/naturepl.com
Inside: © Alex Mustard / naturepl.com (8-9), © David Shale / naturepl.com (10), © Franco Banfi / naturepl.com (11), © David Shale / naturepl.com (12), © David Shale / naturepl.com (16), © Alex Mustard / naturepl.com (16), © Flip Nicklin / naturepl.com (17), © Solvin Zankl / naturepl.com (17), © David Shale / naturepl.com (18), © Franco Banfi / naturepl.com (18), © Solvin Zankl / naturepl.com (19), © David Shale / naturepl.com (20), © David Shale / naturepl.com (21), © Juergen Freund / naturepl.com (22), © Philip Stephen / naturepl.com (23), © Solvin Zankl / naturepl.com (24-25)

This book is rated as: Turquoise Band (Guided Reading)

Into the Deep

Contents

Introduction	6
The Sunlight Zone	8
The Twilight Zone	10
The Midnight Zone	11
The Abyss	12
The Trenches	13
Extreme Places	14
Deep Sea Creatures	16
Adapting to the Deep Sea	18
Humans in the Deep	20
Exploration	20
Destruction	22
Protection	24
Quiz	28
Index/Glossary	30

INCOMING MESSAGE

Dear Finn and Zeek,

I come from a water planet and we hear that the Earth's deep seas are beautiful.

I wonder if you could tell us a bit more about them?

From,
Osmo *(Planet Aquata)*

Introduction

The ocean is enormous! It takes up most of the Earth's surface: about 70%. The deepest part of the ocean has hardly been explored by humans.

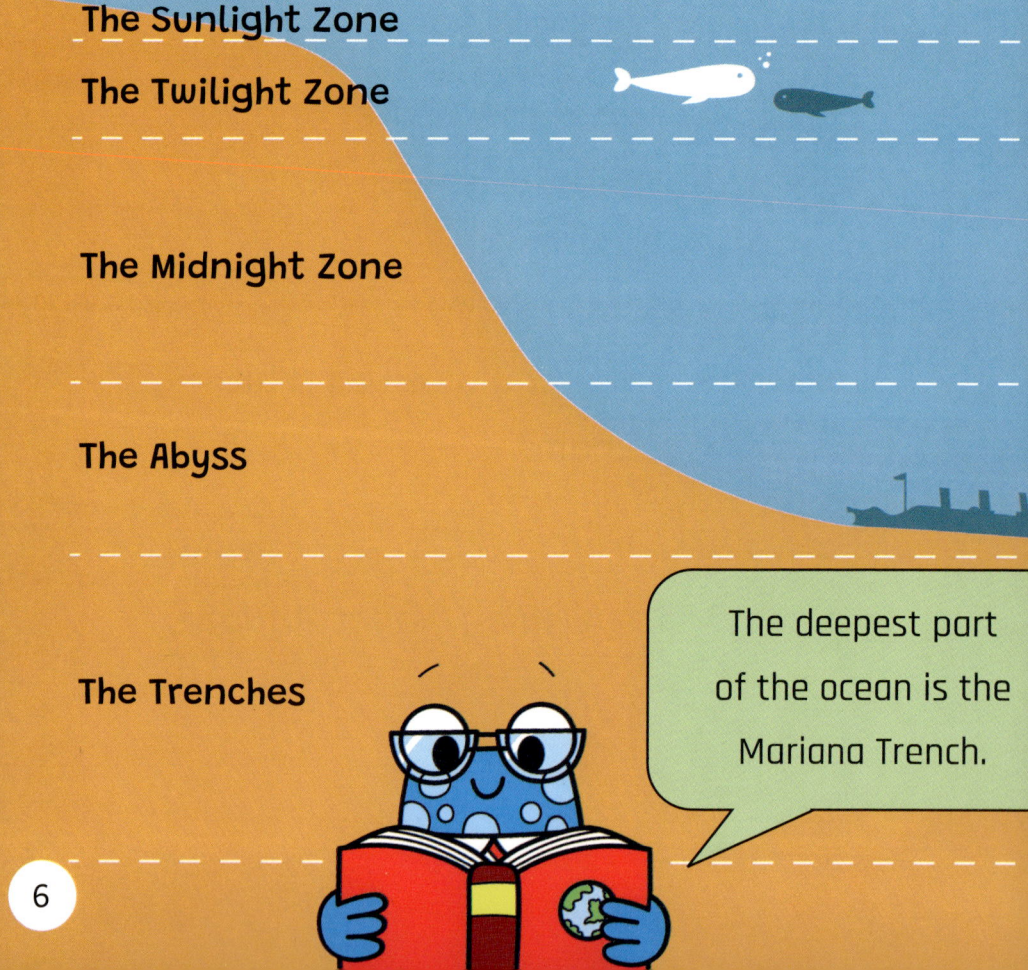

The Sunlight Zone
The Twilight Zone
The Midnight Zone
The Abyss
The Trenches

The deepest part of the ocean is the Mariana Trench.

There are different layers to the ocean, with different parts of the ocean going down to different depths.

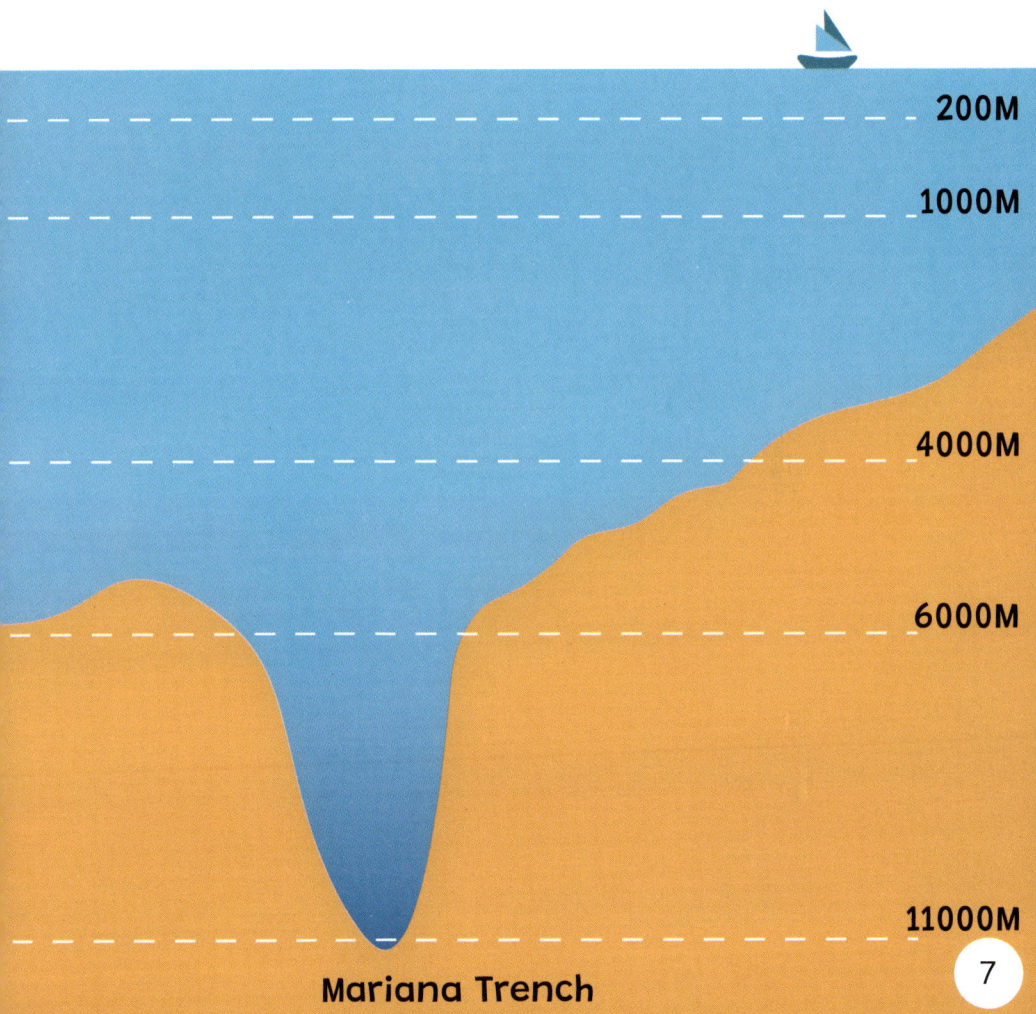

The Sunlight Zone

Up to 200m deep

This is the top layer of the ocean. It is called the Sunlight Zone because it is where the sunlight reaches to.

This makes it a very **habitable** place for sea creatures such as sharks, dolphins and seals. There is also lots of plant life here that needs sunlight to grow.

The Sunlight Zone is the most explored part of the ocean.

The Twilight Zone   200 - 1000m deep

Unlike the Sunlight Zone, no plant life grows in the Twilight Zone as there is little or no light. However, there is still lots of animal life.

Some fish that live here make their own light called '**bioluminescence**' [see page 19].

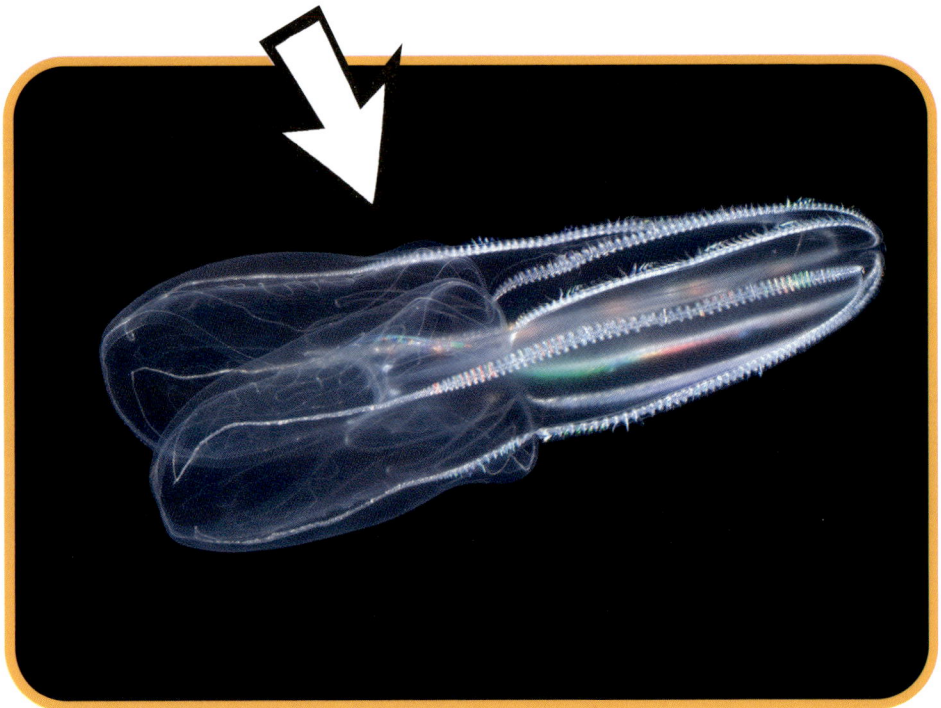

1000 - 4000m deep

The Midnight Zone

This zone has no light at all!

The Titanic sank to this zone (3800m deep).

The Titanic sank in 1912.

Sperm whales have been known to dive this deep!

Sperm whales

The Abyss
4000 – 6000m deep

It's not easy for things to live in this part of the sea. It is very dark and cold.

Deep sea cucumber

The creatures that live here are usually **invertebrates**. This means they have no backbone. Many of the fish down here live on or close to the seabed.

6000 - 11000m+ deep

The Trenches

On the ocean floor, there are some narrow v-shaped holes that go even deeper! These are called trenches. Very few things live at this depth.

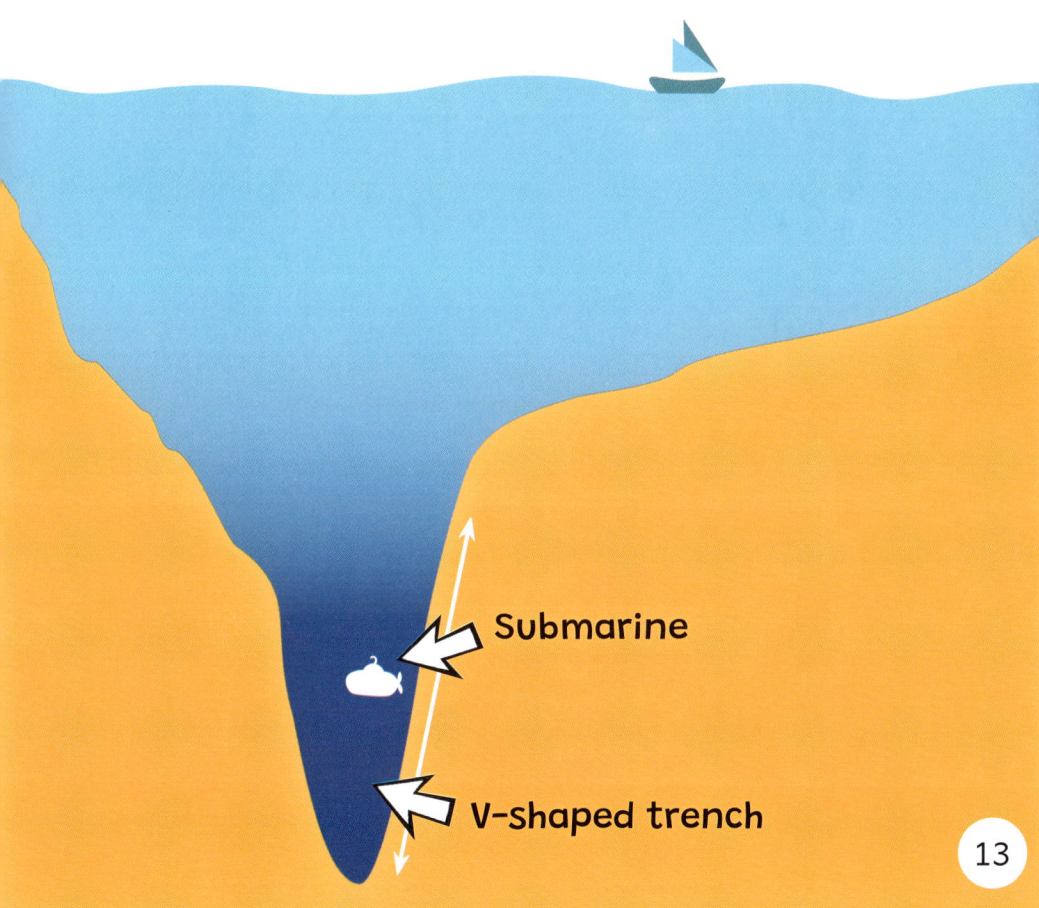

Extreme Places

Hydrothermal Vents

Hydrothermal vents look like underwater volcanoes but release hot water, not lava. When cold sea water gets into deep cracks in the seabed, hot rock underground heats up the sea water and pushes it back out in a jet.

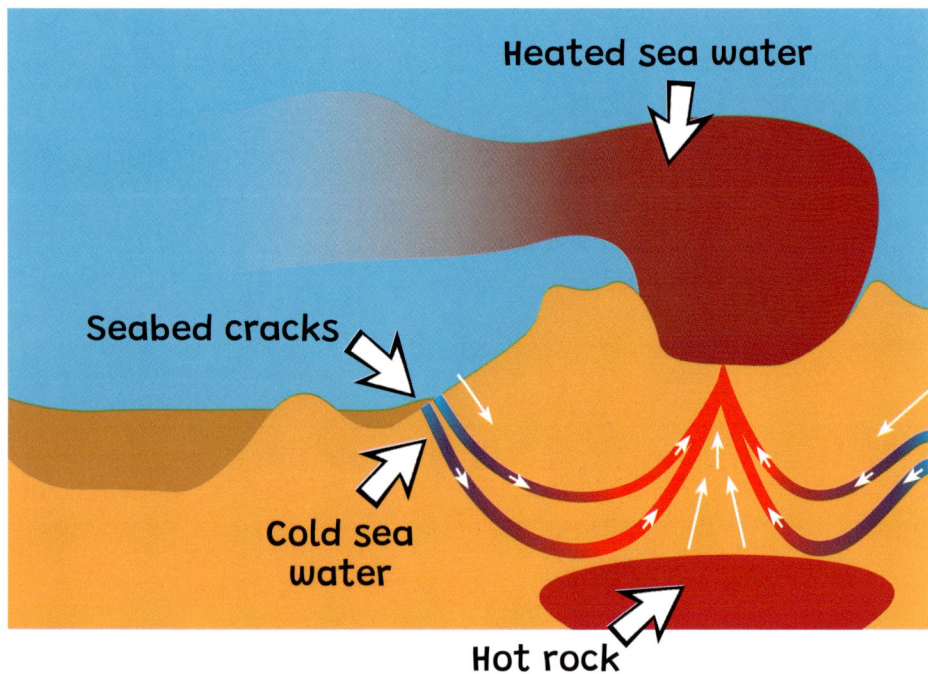

Cold Seeps

Cold seeps are pools of liquid and gas which form near cracks in the seabed. They can be hundreds of meters wide. They are full of chemicals which help creatures in the deep sea to live.

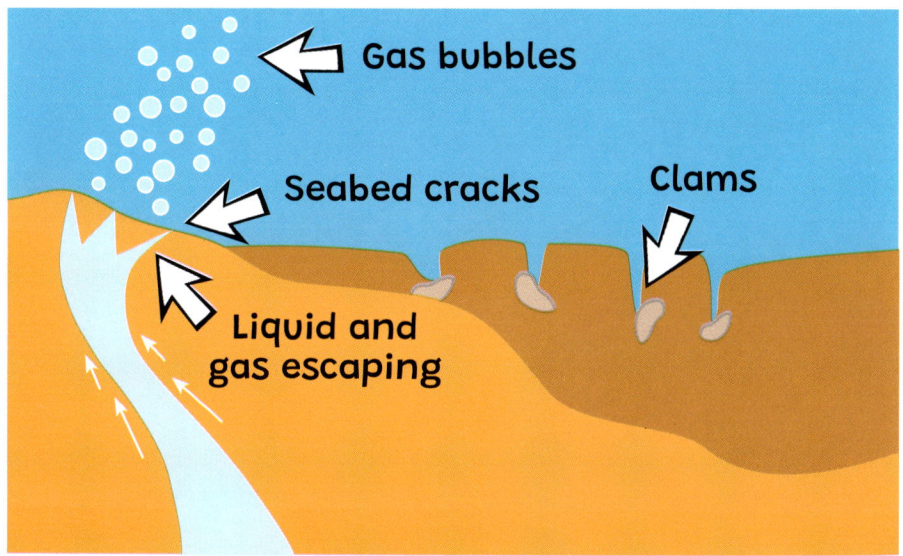

Hydrothermal vents and cold seeps are home to many different creatures. They are important to the ocean's **ecosystem**.

Deep Sea Creatures

Anglerfish

Named after the 'fishing pole' on its head that attracts prey into its mouth.

Whitemargin stargazer

Buries itself in sand and then surprises its prey with an electric shock!

Sea butterfly

A type of sea snail. It is an important food for other creatures.

Cock-eyed squid

This squid has a normal size right eye, but its left eye is double the size!

Adapting to the Deep Sea

Deep sea creatures have to adapt to the cold and dark.

Glass squid

Changing Colour

In the deep sea, most creatures are black, red or transparent to blend in.

Greenland shark

Slow and Steady

Life moves slowly in the deep. The Greenland shark can take over 100 years to fully grow up!

Bioluminescence

In the dark, some creatures of the deep use a **chemical reaction** to create their own light.

Firefly squid

They may do this to...

- Find food

- Attract a mate

- Attract prey to them

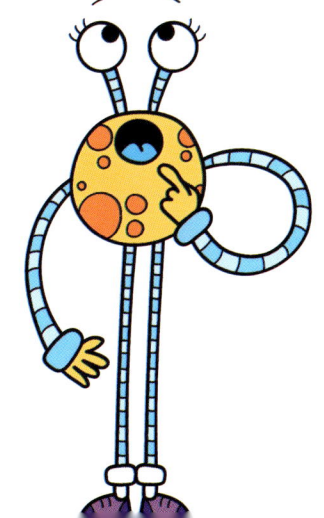

Humans in the Deep

Exploration

Humans use vehicles to explore the deep sea.

**ROV
(Remote Operated Vehicle)**

These vehicles are controlled by computers on the ocean surface. ROVs take photos and collect samples from the deep.

HOV
(Human Operated Vehicle)

These vehicles allow humans to visit the deep sea. They have to be very strong or the pressure would crush them.

Humans in the Deep Destruction

Deep sea fishing is a danger to many types of sea creatures. It can remove too many creatures and damage the ecosystem.

Rubbish has been found in the deepest part of the ocean. Over time, plastic breaks down into tiny, harmful pieces that can be eaten by fish.

Deep sea rigs are used to **mine** oil and gas. This disturbs the ocean bed and causes a lot of **pollution**.

In 2010, there was a huge oil spill at a rig called Deepwater Horizon, near Mexico. The spill killed a lot of sea life.

Humans in the Deep | Protection

There are many things humans can do to help protect the deep sea.

Learn more about the deep sea.

Reduce rubbish by reusing and **recycling**.

Respect nature and don't litter!

Help with beach clean-ups.

Try to use less energy.

Use **clean energy**, instead of oil and gas.

MESSAGE SENT

Dear Osmo,

The deep sea has lots of zones to explore. However, it would be best to check that you are able to cope with the cold and dark before journeying down there.

From,
Finn and Zeek :)

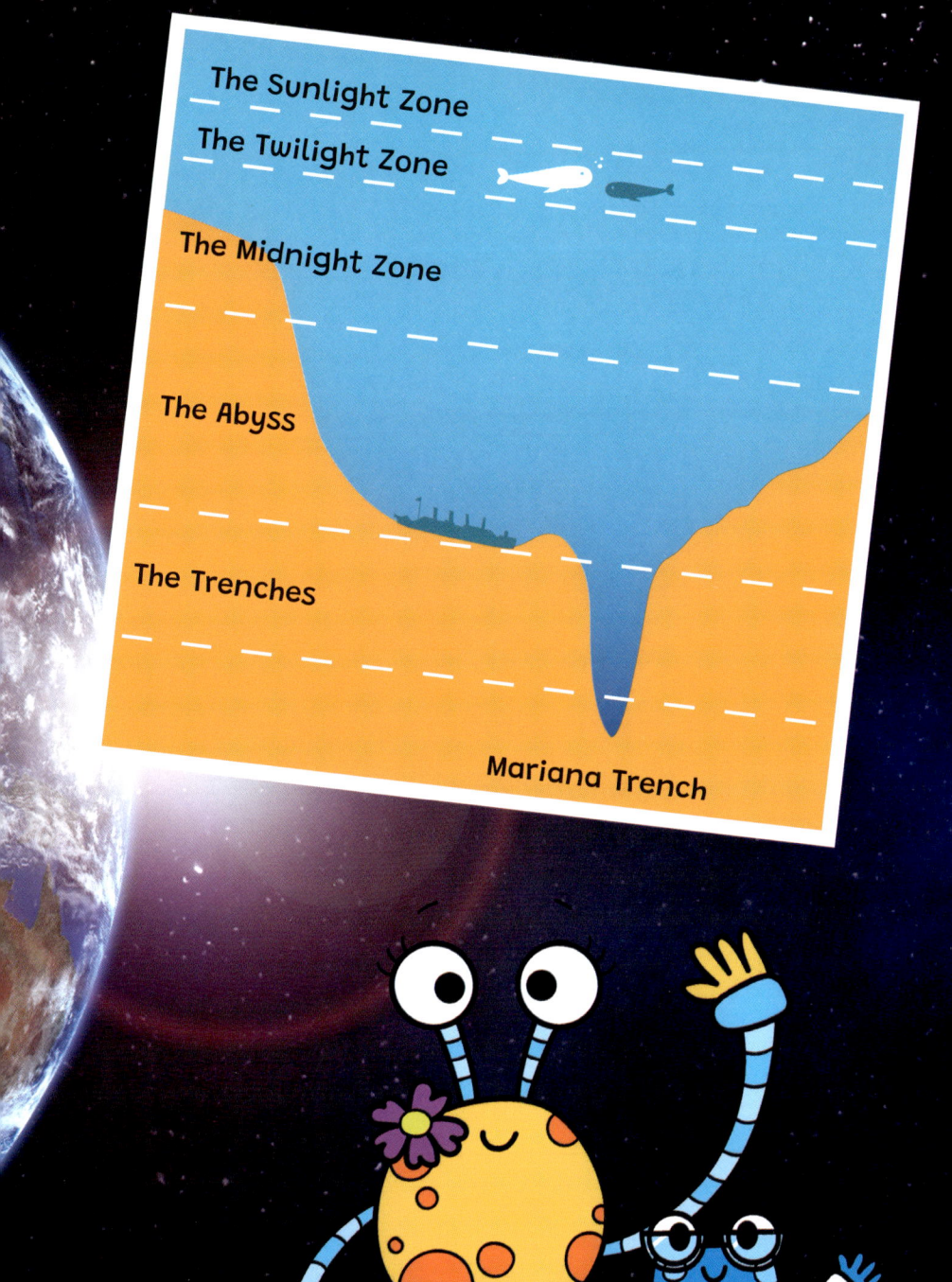

Quiz

1. The ocean makes up roughly how much of the Earth's surface?
a) 50%
b) 70%
c) 90%

2. What is the top layer of the ocean called?
a) The Twilight Zone
b) The Bright Zone
c) The Sunlight Zone

3. What are the v-shaped holes on the ocean floor called?
a) Trenches
b) Deep Zones
c) Mariana Dips

4. What fish has a 'fishing pole' on its head?
a) A fishing fish
b) A hook shark
c) An anglerfish

5. What does HOV stand for?
a) Happy Operated Vehicle
b) Hopping On Vehicles
c) Human Operated Vehicle

6. What are deep sea rigs used for?
a) Mining
b) Exploring
c) Research

Index/Glossary

Bioluminescence pg 10, 19
When a living creature creates its own light with a chemical reaction.

Chemical reaction pg 19
When a substance reacts with another to create something new or different than before.

Clean energy pg 25
Energy which is made from resources that nature will replace, like wind, water and sunshine. It makes little to no pollution.

Ecosystem pg 15, 22
A natural environment and everything that lives in it.

Habitable pg 9
Somewhere that is capable of being lived in.

Quiz Answers:

1. b, 2. c, 3. a, 4. c, 5. c, 6. a

Invertebrates pg 12

Creatures without a backbone in their body.

Mine (mining) pg 23

The process of removing things from the ground.

Pollution pg 23

When harmful materials are released into the environment.

Recycling pg 24

Turning rubbish into something new.

The Titanic pg 11

This ship was built in 1912. At the time it was the largest ship in the world. It sank when it crashed into an iceberg.

Book Bands for Guided Reading

The Institute of Education book banding system is a scale of colours that reflects the various levels of reading difficulty. The bands are assigned by taking into account the content, the language style, the layout and phonics. Word, phrase and sentence level work is also taken into consideration.

Maverick Early Readers are a bright, attractive range of books covering the pink to white bands. All of these books have been book banded for guided reading to the industry standard and edited by a leading educational consultant.

Fiction

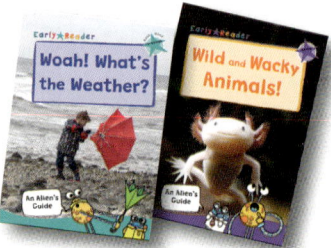

Non-fiction

To view the whole Maverick Readers scheme, visit our website at www.maverickearlyreaders.com

Or scan the QR code above to view our scheme instantly!